ROSSY ZAPATA

THE BOOK OF 100 DRAGONS

LEVEL 2

A FANTASY-THEMED COLORING BOOK

Illustrations and dragon designs: Rossy Zapata
Editorial design: Rossy Zapata
Cleanup: Arminda González Escobedo
Sonia Treviño Luna

PAGE SAMPLES

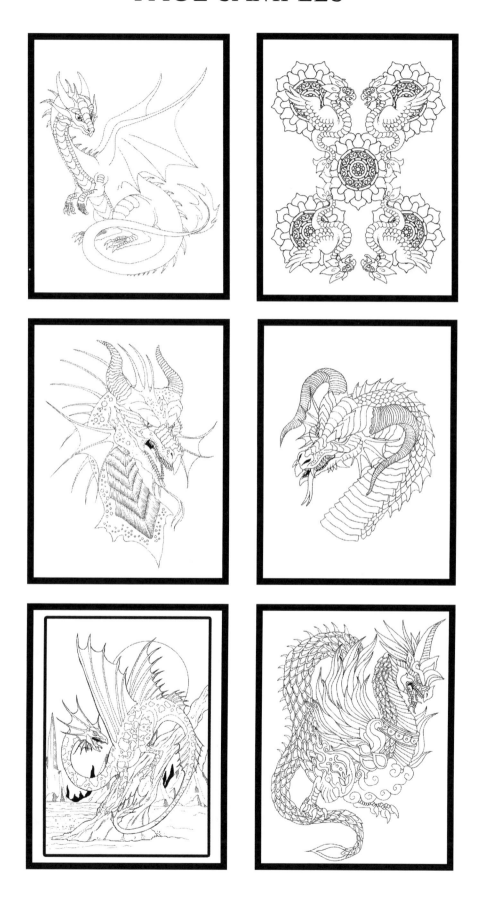

PAGE SAMPLES

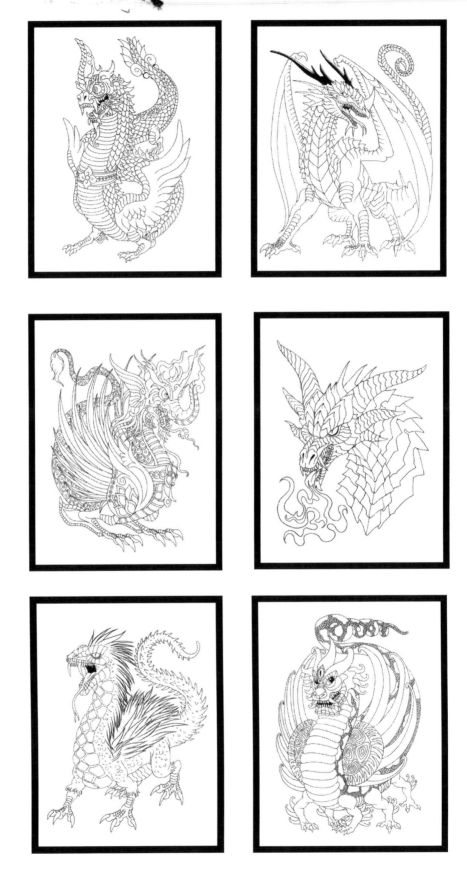

THIS BOOK BELONGS TO:

_____

XiUHCOATL- "FIRE SNAKE"
(MEXICO)

VIVERNA
(ITALY)

TAIWANESE DRAGON

KIRIN
(JAPAN)

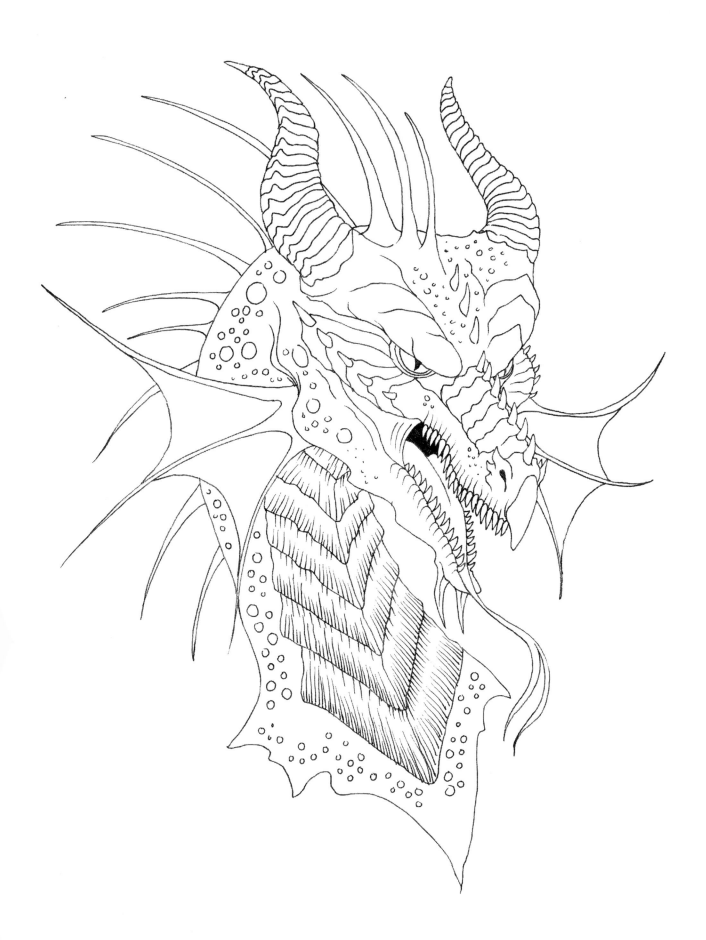

AMPHISBAENA
(GREECE)

NAGA
(THAILAND)

MINOKAWA
(PHILIPPINES)

WINGED LINDWORM
(NORTHERN EUROPE)

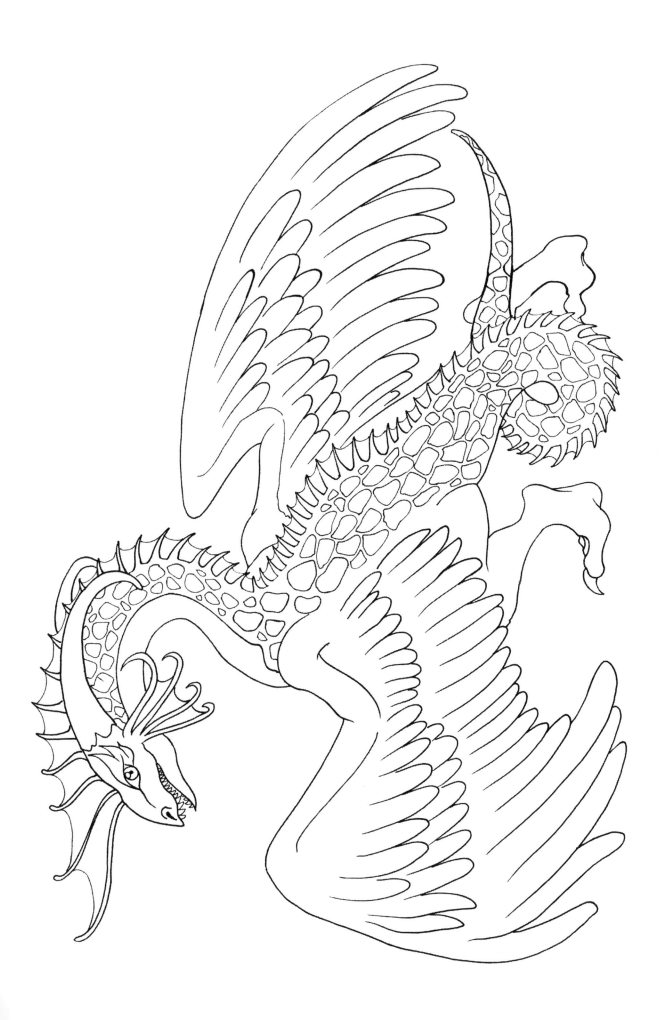

ALEBRIJE DRAGON
(MEXICO)

ZILANT
(RUSSIA)

ZMEY GORYNYCH
(RUSSIA AND UKRAINE)

ANTABOGA
(JAVA, INDONESIA)

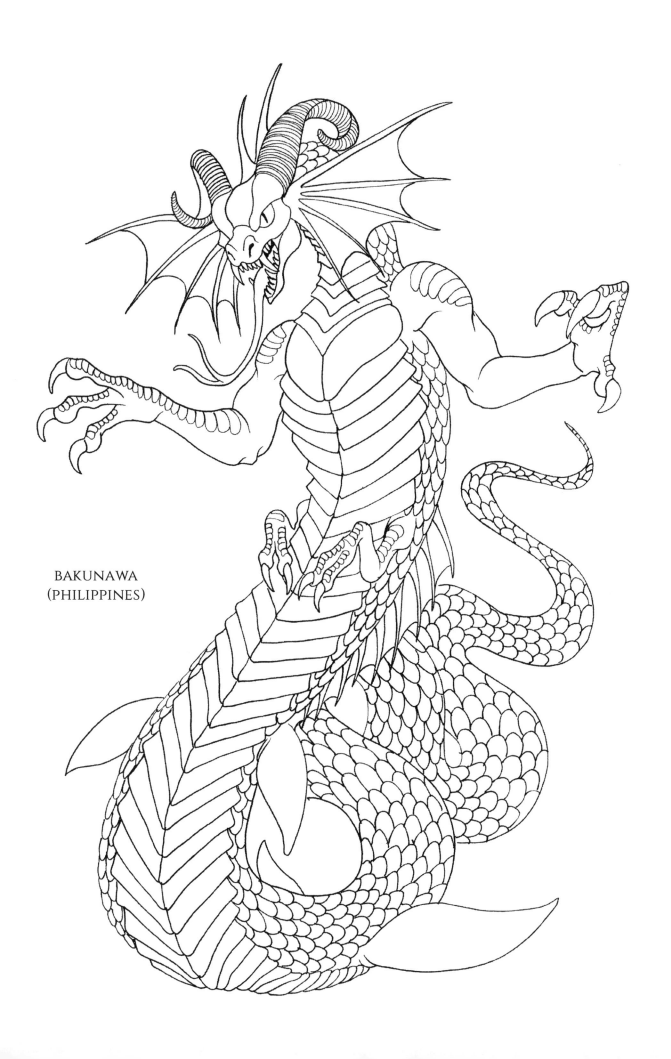

BAKUNAWA
(PHILIPPINES)

ALEBRIJE DRAGON
(MEXICO)

LA TARASQUE
(FRANCE)

LA VELUE
(FRANCE)

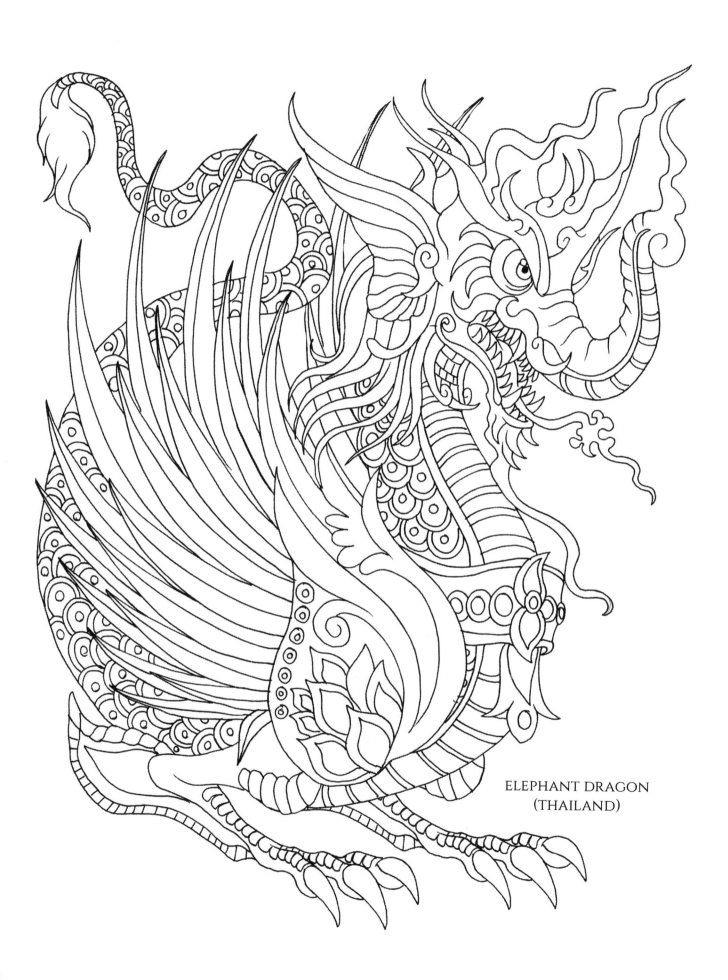

ELEPHANT DRAGON
(THAILAND)

CHINESE DRAGON

ENGLISH DRAGON

AMMIT
(EGYPT)

WYVERN

AMPHIPTERE

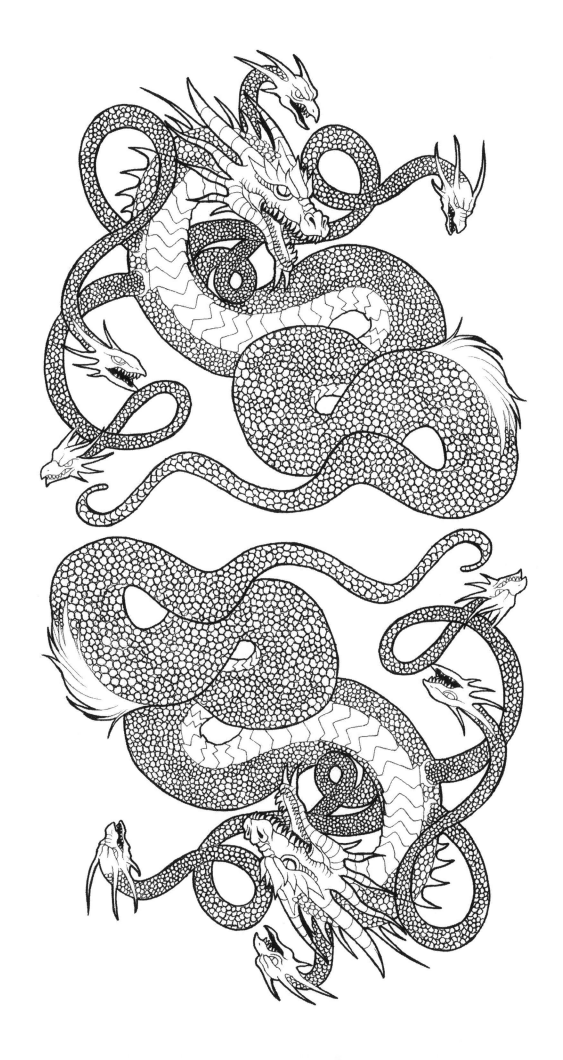

QUETZALCOATL
(MEXICO)

LA TARASQUE
(FRANCE)

YINGLONG
(CHINA)

XIUHCOATL
(MEXICO)

APEP
(EGYPT)

BHUTANESE
DRAGON

BALINESE DRAGON

COCKATRICE

BHUTANESE DRAGON

PERSIAN DRAGON

Made in the USA
Middletown, DE
11 November 2018